SCHOLASTIC

TRUE OR FALSE

Pets

BY MELVIN AND GILDA BERGER

Text copyright © 2009 by Melvin and Gilda Berger
All rights reserved. Published by Scholastic Inc., *Publishers since 1920.*
SCHOLASTIC and associated logos are trademarks and /or
registered trademarks of Scholastic Inc.

ISBN-13: 978-0-545-00396-4
ISBN-10: 0-545-00396-2

10 9 8 7 6 5 4 3 2 1   09 10 11 12 13

Printed in the U.S.A.   23
First printing, April 2009
Book design by Nancy Sabato

Dogs were the first pets. TRUE OR FALSE?

TRUE! Dogs were the first animals to be tamed.

Thousands of years ago, early humans started to raise and care for wolf pups. Over many years, these wolves changed. They became the first dogs. Early people put the dogs to work for them. Some used dogs to herd their sheep. Others trained the dogs to help them hunt and to guard their homes. And many just loved them as pets.

Today's dogs are like wolves in many ways.

Dogs always have wet noses.

TRUE OR FALSE?

FALSE! Dogs don't always have wet noses.

Some healthy dogs have noses that are warm and dry. Most of the time, dogs lick their noses to make them moist. But, wet-nosed or dry-nosed, every dog has an amazing sense of smell. That's because a dog's nose has more than 200 million scent cells, while most humans have only 5 million scent cells on their noses.

Dogs can pick up smells that you do not even notice.

Some dogs have two coats of fur. TRUE OR FALSE?

TRUE!

Some dogs have two coats—an outer coat and an inner coat. Dogs that live in cold climates have two coats of fur. The outer coat is like a poncho. It protects the animal from ice and snow. Most dogs have a thin, light coat during the summer and a heavier coat in the winter. They shed their winter coats in the spring and grow new ones in the fall.

A dog's body temperature is about 5 degrees higher than your temperature.

Bloodhounds can only follow the smell of blood.

TRUE OR FALSE?

FALSE! Bloodhounds can track many different smells.

A bloodhound has an exceptional sense of smell. It walks or runs along with its nose close to the ground. The pointed nose picks up every smell that people or animals leave as they pass by. The dog's long, droopy ears help bring the scents from the ground to its nose. A well-trained bloodhound can follow a trail that is two to three days old.

Some think the dog got its name from the expression *blooded hound*, which refers to a hound of pure breeding.

Dogs and cats are natural enemies.

TRUE
OR
FALSE?

FALSE! Dogs and cats can be great friends.

Cats' fear of dogs probably comes from generations of cats being chased by dogs. Many cats will arch their backs and hiss when they meet a strange dog. And dogs will often growl and bark at unfamiliar cats. But pet dogs and cats often get along very well. Mother cats have nursed motherless puppies. And dogs have been known to wash newborn kittens.

Dogs and cats can also learn to live with pet rabbits and birds.

Cats can see in the dark. TRUE OR FALSE?

FALSE! Cats have amazing eyes, but they cannot see in total darkness.

Cats need some light to be able to see. In dim light, their pupils open very wide. This lets lots of light enter. The dim light strikes the back surface of the eye. This back surface acts like a mirror. It reflects the light back to make it brighter. It also makes cats' eyes gleam when struck by light rays in the dark.

A cat sees about six times better in dim light than you do.

House cats hate to take baths. TRUE OR FALSE?

TRUE!

Most cats hate being dunked into water.

Actually, many cats do not mind getting wet. But they must be the ones to decide whether or not to take a bath. Being picked up and dunked into a tub of water hurts a cat's feelings. But even cats that hate taking baths keep very clean. A cat washes its face by licking a paw and then rubbing it around. And it cleans its body by licking its fur.

Cats can swim—even though most don't like getting wet.

Cats only scratch on posts to sharpen their claws.

TRUE OR FALSE?

FALSE! Cats have other reasons for scratching.

Scratching on posts helps a cat spread its claws open. This lets the cat remove any dirt that's stuck there. Scratching also helps the cat stretch its body and exercise its leg muscles. And scratching leaves the cat's smell on the post, marking it as the cat's property. Of course, while all this is going on, the cat is also sharpening its claws.

A cat has four claws on each of its hind paws and five claws on each of its front paws.

Cats can eat dog food.

TRUE
OR
FALSE?

FALSE! Cats Should only eat cat food.

Dog food is not good for cats because it has too little protein. Cats need five times more protein than dogs do. Cats should eat foods that are rich in protein, especially beef, chicken, liver, heart, kidney, and fish. A high-protein diet helps them grow healthy and strong. Cats should only be given milk occasionally.

A steady menu of dog food may cause a cat to go blind.

A cat lying low is ready to attack. **TRUE OR FALSE?**

TRUE!

A cat's low crawl tells you it's about to attack. A cat's body language can tell you a lot about the animal's mood. A cat lying flat or crawling close to the ground may be saying, "I'm about to pounce." In the same way, a cat rubbing itself against your leg can mean "I love you." A tail fully erect always says, "Glad to see you!"

An arched back usually means "Leave me alone."

Parakeets like to live alone.

TRUE OR FALSE?

FALSE! Parakeets enjoy having company.

Pet parakeets are small- to medium-size parrots. In the wild, they live in huge, noisy flocks. As pets, they seem to like the company of people and other parakeets. Parakeets are loving birds and need to be noticed and talked to. If you hear a parakeet making *ack-ack* sounds, that means the parakeet is content. *Fweep*, though, signals fear or distress.

Lovebirds are curious, playful, cuddly parrots.

Parakeets
can learn to
speak. **TRUE**
OR
FALSE?

TRUE! You can teach a parakeet to speak and answer questions.

Most parakeets can learn to say at least a few words. Males, though, seem to learn faster than females. If you want to teach a bird to speak, start when the bird is very young. Repeat a word over and over again. Speak slowly and loudly. After the parakeet learns that word, you can go on to teach it other words.

The record vocabulary for a parakeet is more than 1,700 words.

All canaries are bright yellow. **TRUE** OR **FALSE?**

FALSE! Pet canaries may also be white, orange, brown, dark green, gray, red, or mixed colors.

There are several kinds, or breeds, of canaries. All male canaries sing. They are named for the sound of their songs. The roller sounds like a flute and trills with an almost-closed beak. The chopper has a wilder song. It sings with its head thrown back and its beak wide open.

The popular American canary combines the songs of the roller and the chopper.

Canaries only eat seeds.

TRUE OR FALSE?

FALSE! Canaries do not only eat seeds.

Canaries do like seeds best of all. But, in the wild, canaries also eat insects. At home, they can get protein from chopped-up hard-boiled eggs. Canaries also enjoy broccoli, corn, yams, lettuce, carrots, apples, oranges, and bananas. Prepared canary food may consist of nuts, seeds, vegetables, and fruits.

A bit of cayenne pepper added to birdseed gives a yellow canary's feathers a deeper color.

Hamsters have big, fat cheeks.

TRUE OR FALSE?

FALSE! Most of the time, a hamster's cheeks are not chubby.

A hamster crams its food into its mouth. Inside its cheeks are big bags, or pouches, which can stretch and hold lots of food. When full, the pouches stick out to the sides. The hamster's face looks round and fat. Then the hamster carries the food in its pouches to a safe place for eating. Or it buries the food for later.

When frightened, a mother hamster hides her newborn pups in her cheek pouches.

Hamsters are vegetarians. TRUE OR FALSE?

FALSE! In addition to plant foods, hamsters eat insects and other small creatures.

Hamsters eat an amazing amount of food. A feast for a hamster can include grains, apples, sweet potatoes, carrots, corn, and cooked meat. Dog biscuits are also very good for pet hamsters. Chewing or gnawing on dog biscuits helps hamsters trim their teeth—or else they will just keep growing longer and longer.

Never feed a hamster sweets—especially not chocolate.

Hamsters like to hide. **TRUE** or **FALSE?**

TRUE! Most hamsters feel safe in tight, narrow, dark places.

In the wild, hamsters spend lots of time in tunnels they dig in the ground. That's where they go to escape their enemies. Their favorite sleeping places in home cages are cardboard tubes or small containers. They make good "tunnels" for pet hamsters. Hamsters are generally wide awake at night and sleepy during the day.

Today's pet hamsters come from wild ancestors captured in 1930.

Gerbils have longer tails than hamsters. **TRUE OR FALSE?**

TRUE! Gerbils are about the same size as hamsters but with much longer tails.

A gerbil has a long, furry tail and narrow back feet. It looks like a mouse, but it jumps around like a tiny kangaroo. Wild gerbils live in dry, sandy deserts. As pets, gerbils love to clean themselves in dust, not in water. This makes their fur smoother and shinier. Gerbils dig, jump, climb, and chew—just like hamsters.

A gerbil's tail is about as long as its body.

Gerbils don't like to be held.

TRUE OR FALSE?

FALSE! Gerbils are very friendly animals.

Gerbils seem to like people. They are very gentle with them. When you lift a gerbil from its cage, it will usually sit quietly in your hand. It will let you pet its soft fur. You may hear it squeak. Sometimes you can feel that the gerbil is purring, even though you cannot hear it. Soon the gerbil will be climbing all over you.

Sometimes gerbils do not get along with other gerbils in the same cage.

Guinea pigs
are in the
pig family.

TRUE
OR
FALSE?

FALSE! Guinea pigs are cousins of hamsters and gerbils, not pigs.

Like hamsters and gerbils, guinea pigs mainly eat plants. This includes seeds, and also some grains such as corn and wheat. Many guinea pig owners feed their pet pellets, hay, carrot tops, and apple slices. Some guinea pigs have a tendency to overeat, so watch how much you feed them.

A baby guinea pig is called a pup.

Rabbits like to be picked up by their ears.

TRUE OR FALSE?

FALSE! Holding a rabbit by its ears hurts the animal.

You should use both hands to pick up your rabbit—one hand to support the chest and the other to support the bottom. Many rabbits don't like to be picked up, so be careful and gentle.

Rabbits cannot walk or run, but they can surely hop.

All goldfish look alike.

TRUE OR FALSE?

FALSE! Goldfish come in many different shapes and colors.

Goldfish are the most popular pet fish. The smallest are no more than 2 inches (5.1 centimeters) long. The biggest goldfish can reach 18 inches (45.7 centimeters) or more in length. Their fins also vary greatly in size and shape. Although many goldfish are gold, some are red, orange, brown, black, or even white. All together there are about 100 kinds of domestic goldfish in the world.

Goldfish lose their color if kept in dim light.

Index